A PLUM ISLAND YEAR

A
PLUM
ISLAND
YEAR

Peggy Laufer

TITCOMB STREET PRESS
Newburyport, Massachusetts 2016

Newburyport, Massachusetts 2016

*For my Mom
and my diverse,
fantastic family*

They are my ocean.

And in memory of

*my father, Harry
my friend, Marlene
my dog, Daisy*

Good Morning, Children
Good Morning, Mrs. Laufer

For forty years, this is how my day began. I taught
young school children until I retired in 2014. In the
year after I stopped teaching I continued to wake
early, lonely for my children. For the first time since
I was very young, I had no work, few responsibilities,
time for all kinds of space in my thinking, thinking in
my space. So I took my early morning loneliness and
energy and freedom to Plum Island. It's a place I love,
and it's close. Mostly I just showed up. I put myself
there and looked around and wrote down what I saw.
This book contains some of the poems from that year.
They chaperoned me through the loss of my children
and the enormous loss of my father. My time at Plum
Island became my morning meeting.

Good Morning, Ocean
Good Morning, Peggy

Contents

Intro

Contents

In the clarity of morning
I am the poet I have always been.
I see the ice
I breathe cool air.

Then I go home and feed the dogs.

A PLUM ISLAND YEAR

No Poem

I drove to Plum Island early,
a little piece of paper
in my pocket,
to see if I could write a poem.
Before I even got where I was going
I saw a big snowy owl
surveying the marshes
from a telephone pole
and I saw his eyes
when his head turned toward me.

On the refuge,
pretty quick,
I saw the northern harrier.
I was heading south,
she north,
so the encounter was brief.
But I saw her.
And then the turkeys walking the road,
a small flock with a leader.
At the swamp
I had to turn around.
The road was closed for mud.

Going back
I stopped to watch the turkeys
and so did a lady with a camera.
When she opened her door
and put her feet on the road,
big turkey chased
and camera lady left
and I liked it.

Almost to the gatehouse
I looked with binoculars
at another white owl.
It was big
and it was great,
neck whirling to scan
the tidal river.

Leaving, I saw, again,
the first owl on the telephone pole
still looking,
no care for the cars
or the people stopped to see.
I drove the turnpike home.

No poem though.

Sabbath Year

After working forty years
rising early for time alone
before days filled with children
and what they might teach me,
now is the Sabbath year.
A Sunday without a Monday looming.
Three hundred and sixty-five Sundays.

And what do you do on the Sabbath?
Give thanks, calm down, ponder God,
appreciate family.
Take long walks, look for birds,
slowly disconnect
and remember with an open hand.

So much snow in February.

Birds Without Coats

The raptors at the mouth
of the Merrimac
show winter
for what it really is.

Eagles, harriers and snowy owls,
feathers blow in cold winds.
Hawks weave through town,
scan white and brown lands
for movement and life,
live the desolation of February.

Warm in my white down bed
comforted by dogs and man,
not hungry,
I think of those fierce birds,
birds without coats,
hungry each day,
harsh and focused
on making it through.

Ice Baby Blue

The ice lay like fabric
on the marsh.
You could see low tide
had sunk the water
and left that sheet of ice
to shift or slide,
quiet gravity
pulling toward the center.

Sky and sun
turn the ice baby blue
as it waits
for the rise of the tide,
the tug of the moon.

Birthday Harrier

I could imagine it's for me,
this aerial dance of happiness,
such skill and agility,
the freedom of the skies
to twist and turn
or hover and drop.

I know she's hungry,
but still.
It could be my birthday present.
It could be Harry sharing some joy.
It could be an offering for the coming year.

And then I see her mate
cruising low
and I know it will be
about love.

Contemplating Poets

Up since five
to get to Plum Island.
Sunrise over the ocean,
moonset over the marsh.
Love those purple brambles
The snow is almost gone.
Robin up and singing,
redwing found a mate.
Snowy owl #100
sitting lumpy on the marsh
wondering
what happened
to the lemmings,
what happened to the airplanes,
wondering.

Woodcock

Woodcock in the bushes,
Thump, thump, thump, thump—
Slow—not concerned.

For Marlene

Maybe a prairie chicken?
There used to be a lot of them.
Looks like good eatin',
Runs like a chicken.

Gray-patched head,
cameo disappearing
into dried sticks, grasses, brush.
My friend the birder says:
Don't talk about it.

Harry

I see the harrier fly low
and love it so much
so much it hurts
and goes to my father.

Being left
the freedom to fly
sometimes I feel
I have nothing to say

Except to him.

Shhhh

Now the robins don't fly
As I creep by
In my camouflage blue
They don't even shoo!

Rain

An unexpected gift
of rain
changed everything:
The smells,
the sound of my tires on dirt.
Even the water looks different
accepting its heaven.

I see through drops on my glasses
feel the water on my face.
I bet if I sat here all day
still and looking
I'd see my meadow green up.

April.

Female with Nest and One Egg

An errant duck today,
female mallard
lost or looking.
Saw her twice,
coming and going.

Cloud Ocean

The snow tried,
but grass shows through anyway.
The cloudbank east
tricks my eyes:
I think the ocean
has moved closer.

Then I understand.

It's the storm
riding on the sea
that changes everything,
again.
I see the cloud ocean
through the dunes.
The river right there, too.

The exact opposite
of being between a rock
and a hard place.

The Short-Tailed Weasel

Oh my God!
I saw a weasel.
She was brown,
white under,
not too big,
long though,
mouse
dangling
from her mouth.

Right About Now

Right about now
I think there will be no poem today.
The windmills and
the flats frozen still.
I'm going 18 miles per hour
on the ride home from Hellcat
and then Glenn tells the story:
If he listens,
he can hear the peepers
on Wild Lake,
sounds from when he was a boy,
a little miracle in his head.

Tom of Plum Island

A trunculated robin,
he told me.
After that every time I saw him
I knew
he knew something good,
exotic,
hard to pronounce.

One morning I felt
brave enough to interrupt.
He answered,
Just listening to fox sparrows,
always love them.

Today

Today the carp in the north pool
were flipping in the shallows.

I watched the woodcock cross the road.
It took twenty minutes!

The Catbird

The catbird says a lot of things
as she sits puffed up
on the sassafras tree,
singing everyone's songs.
Beautiful gray,
black crown,
patch of red
shows me everything.
Spikes my morning
like a shot of tequila.

Past Hellcat

The bump of the road
The fuzz of the rain
The hum in my body
The calm of my heart
The quiet of the place
The slowing of my car
The greeting of the birds

Fish after Fish after Fish

Trying so hard to be here now
I take the dawn ride to Plum Island.
Tangerine sunrise
over cobalt water
begins to get me there.
Sky blue pink
my new favorite color.

I see a lone bird,
a cormorant, maybe,
fishing the salt pans.
She has found a stellar spot.
She scoots along the surface
head down, mouth open,
full speed ahead
catching fish after fish
after fish!

Ocean's Edge

So foggy the lights are cotton
The birds are shadows
Walk to low, low tide
Dollars and dimes and scallops
Large, wave-riding loons
Lost in looking
Prayer at ocean's edge.

Sometimes

Sometimes, the sound of waves
lapping the empty shore,
quiet rumble of breakers over the sandbar,
the comfort of turkeys
is what you come for.

Welcoming Morning

On the tallest last tree
at Sandy Point
sits a yellow bird
welcoming morning.
Two swans honk overhead
off to swim in the river.
The small bird is stirred
but not shaken.

Manners

Gull on the stone road,
picking at a mussel from the marsh
just dropped and cracked.
I'll wait.

Gull eats mussel,
walks to post and hops up
to let me pass.
Thank you.
Thank you.

Minus Degrees Fahrenheit

Quiet
Still
No cars
But mine
Iced puddles
Frozen surface
North pool
Empty nest
Looks cold
Is cold

Chickadees and Harriers

The chickadees call me,
it should be enough.

Then I see the harriers,
two together—first time.
They meet in the air
and dance.

Swooping around
she follows him.
Or he follows her.

Ocean Floor

Streets are quiet and wet.
Men are working in tee shirts.
Stinky smells from the plant.
My head is wrapped in cotton
as I seek the marsh.

I love it after it rains,
everything washed clean,
puddles on the road.

Low, low tide.
Walk the ocean floor.
Know you're sad
when you cry
on the beach.

Watcher

A snowy owl
in black and white
checkered suit,
sits on the boardwalk railing,
waiting, watching
my solitary prayer.
Only when I return
does he lift off and fly
toward Emerson Rocks.

Little Human Light

Morning at the gas station
Oh well.
Sheds a little human light
on the early experience.

Brown dog in the back seat
perfect like cinnamon,
two crooked ears,
white throat,
expectant cookie face.
No cookie, but
admiration
from the gas station guy.

School buses,
dog walkers,
road blocks.

By the time I get to the island
the sun will be so high
I'll need my baseball hat.

Lots of ducks in the river,
big raptor on the pink house
bombarded by crows.

Finally at the island
and through the gates
I think of my warm bed
and my lover whispering,
"Is this what you wanted?"

Yes.

Heron

Big birds.
Cold birds.
Solitude.

I watched a heron
Standing in the north pool
Water up to her belly
Silver head
Neck like a broomstick
Dagger beak
Almost asleep

No!

Like lightning
The dagger grabbed
A big black fish,
Flapped and shook
And turned that fish.
I watched her neck
Get fat and fluffed up.
More shaking

Then quiet
Back to still.
Alert.

I imagined the fish
Flopping in her belly
But heron was ready for the next,
Her neck back to broomstick.

After Vermont's Pointed Firs

After Vermont's pointed firs
and snow-covered maples
and endless forests
and brooks winding through the wilderness,
I find myself at the marsh.

A jay picking at an old caterpillar nest
blowing in the cold.
Scat on the road.
Frost on the dune grass.

Tide going out,
gulls feasting.
Burst bank of sand dollars
at the ocean's edge.

You may not have the
wilderness and pointed firs.
Pay attention to your riches
at the sea.
To find something
you have to go and look.

Peggy Laude
A Plum Island yea

Lord

A snowy owl,
huge,
in a tree,
on a branch like a twig,
Lord of the Marsh.

A message.
A greeting.
Eyes open:
A vision against
the gray sky.

The Refuge Was Quiet

The refuge was quiet
even at low tide.
The big birds
had flown to the turnpike.

Sometimes, I guess,
you just have to
get into town.

Present

Walk in the rain
on the beach.
It's not really like
being lonely.
There's wonder
and birds
and water
and sand.

peggy Laube

Acknowledgments

I have many who I hold in my heart and am thankful for. I would not have been able to create this little book without those who lift me up:

Glenn
Marlon, Julian, Julia
Carolyn and Stephen
Lani and Kyree
Children and Friends